Vocals · Guitar · Keyboa

T0080448

Best of
Spirituals & Gospels

59 Great Songs
Easy Arrangements for 1–2 Voices

ED 9643
ISMN M-001-13541-2

www.schott-music.com

Mainz · London · Madrid · New York · Prag · Paris · Tokyo · Toronto
© 2003 SCHOTT MUSIK INTERNATIONAL GmbH & Co. KG, Mainz · Printed in Germany

Bestell-Nr.: ED 9643
ISMN M-001-13541-2

© 2003 Schott Musik International, Mainz
Vocal Arrangements: Bill Harris
Printed in Germany · BSS 51240

www.schott-music.com

Contents
Inhalt / Contenu

Amazing Grace

Traditional

1. A - maz - ing grace how sweet the sounds, that saved a wretch like me._____ I once was___ lost but now I'm found, was blind but now I see._____

2.
'T was grace that taught my heart to fear,
And grace my fears relieved.
How precious did that grace appear,
The hour I first believed.

3.

When we've been there ten thousand years,
Bright shining as the sun.
We've no less days to sing God's praise,
Than when we first begun.

4.

Through many dangers, toils and snares,
I have already come.
This grace hath brought me safe thus far,
And grace will lead me home.

5.

How sweet the name of Jesus sounds
In a believer's ear.
It soothes his sorrows, heals the wounds,
And drives away his fear.

6.

Must Jesus bear the cross alone
And all the world go free?
No, there's a cross for everyone,
And there's a cross for me.

7.

Yeah, when this flesh and heart shall fail,
And mortal life shall cease,
I shall possess – beyond the veil –
A life of joy and peace.

8.

The world shall soon dissolve like snow,
The sun refuse to shine;
But God who called me here below,
Shall be forever mine.

9.

The Lord has promised good to me,
His word my hope secures,
He will my shield and portion be
As long as life endures.

Amen

Traditional

2. Amen, …
See him in the temple, talking to the Elders,
How they marveled at his wisdom.

3. Amen, …
See him in the garden, praying to his father
In deepest sorrow.

4. Amen, …
Yes, he is my savior, Jesus did to help us,
And he rose on Easter.

5. Amen, …
Hallelujah in the kingdom with my savior,
Amen, Amen.

Deep River

Traditional

Deep____ riv - er, my home is o - ver Jor - dan.

Deep____ riv - er, Lord, I want to cross o - ver in that camp - ground. 1. Oh,

don't you want to__ go__ to that gos - pel feast,__ that

Prom - ised Land,__ where all__ is peace? Deep__

riv - er, Lord, I want to cross o - ver in that camp - ground.

2.
Oh, I'll go up to Heaven
And take my seat.
And cast my crown
At Jesus' feet. Deep River ...

3.
Oh, when I get to Heaven,
I'll walk about,
There's no one there
To turn me out. Deep River ...

And I Couldn't Hear Nobody Pray

Traditional

And I could-n't hear no-bo-dy pray, and I could-n't hear no-bo-dy pray. O way down yon-der by my-self;— and I could-n't hear no-bo-dy pray. 1. And I could-n't hear no-bo-dy pray — in the al-ley— I could-n't hear no-bo-dy pray — on my knees — I could-n't hear no-bo-dy pray — with my bur-den— I could-n't hear no-bo-dy

2.
And I couldn't hear nobody pray – 'n chilly waters –
I couldn't hear nobody pray – in the Jordan –
I couldn't hear nobody pray – crossing over –
I couldn't hear nobody pray – into Canaan –
And I couldn't hear nobody pray …

3.
And I couldn't hear nobody pray – hallelujah –
I couldn't hear nobody pray – troubles over –
I couldn't hear nobody pray – in the kingdom –
I couldn't hear nobody pray – with my Jesus –
And I couldn't hear nobody pray …

Come And Go With Me

Traditional

2.
There ain't no bowing in that land,
Ain't no bowing in that land,
Ain't no bowing in that land where I'm bound.

3.
There ain't no kneeling in that land
Ain't no kneeling in that land,
Ain't no kneeling in that land where I'm bound.

4.
There ain't no poverty in that land
Ain't no poverty in that land,
Ain't no poverty in that land where I'm bound.

5.
 There's love and brotherhood in that land
Love and brotherhood in that land,
Love and brotherhood in that land where I'm bound.

6.
There's peace and freedom in that land
Peace and freedom in that land,
Peace and freedom in that land where I'm bound.

Didn't It Rain?

Traditional

Did - n't it rain, chil - dren,——

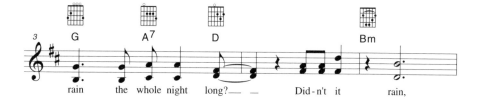

rain the whole night long?—— — Did - n't it rain,

Lord? Did - n't it rain, Lord? Did - n't it rain,

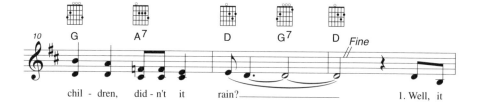

chil - dren, did - n't it rain?———— 1. Well, it

rained   for - ty   days,   for - ty   nights with - out   stop - pin',

No - ah   cried   "Stop!"   but   the   rain   kept   a - drop - pin'.   The

sin - ners clung   to   trees,   they   were   sigh - in'   and   a - sob - bin' when they

heard   them   wa - ters   roar._____   Did - n't   it

D.S. al Fine

2.
Some climbed the mountain, some climbed the hill;
Some started floatin' and a-rowin' with a will.
Some started swimmin', and I guess they're swimmin' still,
Cause they heard them waters roar.

Didn't My Lord Deliver Daniel

Traditional

Did - n't   my Lord de - li - ver   Da - niel,—— de - li - ver

Da - niel,—— de - li - ver Da - niel.—— Did - n't my Lord de - li - ver

Da - niel———— and   why not ev - er - y   man?   Did - n't

man?   1. He de - li - vered Da - niel from the   li - on's   den,

Jo - nah from the bel - ly of the   whale   and the   He - brew chil - dren from the

fi - er - y   fur - nace, and   why not   ev - er - y   man?   *D.C. al Fine*

2.

The moon run down in a purple stream,
And the sun forbear to shine.
And every star will disappear,
King Jesus shall be mine.
Didn't my Lord deliver Daniel,
Deliver Daniel, deliver Daniel.
Didn't my Lord deliver Daniel,
And why not every my man.

3.

The wind blows east and the wind blows west,
It blows like a judgement day.
And every poor soul that never did pray
Will be glad to pray that day.
Didn't my Lord deliver Daniel,
Deliver Daniel, deliver Daniel.
Didn't my Lord deliver Daniel,
And why not every my man.

4.

I set my foot on the Gospel ship,
And the ship began to sail.
And it landed over on Canaan's shore,
And I'll never come back no more.
Didn't my Lord deliver Daniel,
Deliver Daniel, deliver Daniel.
Didn't my Lord deliver Daniel,
And why not every my man.

Down By The Riverside

Traditional

I'm gon-na lay down my bur-den down by the riv-er-side,____ down by the riv-er-side,____ down by the riv-er-side.____ I'm gon-na lay down my bur-den down by the riv-er-side,____ down by the riv-er-side.

I ain't gonna stu-dy____ war no more,____

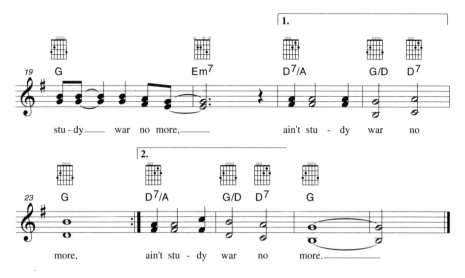

2.
I'm gonna lay down my sword and shield
Down by the riverside …
… Ain't study war no more.

3.
I'm gonna put on my travelin' shoes
Down by the riverside …
… Ain't study war no more.

4.
I'm gonna put on my long white rope
Down by the riverside …
… Ain't study war no more.

5.
I'm gonna put on my starry crown
Down by the riverside …
… Ain't study war no more.

Dry Bones

Traditional

Go, Tell It On The Mountains

Traditional

2.
Go, tell it ...
When I was a sinner,
I prayed both night and day.
I asked my Lord to help me
And he showed me the way.

3.
Go, tell it ...
He made me a watchman
Upon the city-wall,
And if I am a Christian
I am the least of all.

4.
Go, tell it ...
'T was in a lowly manger
That Jesus Christ was born.
The Lord sent down an angel
That bright and glorious morn'.
Go, tell it on ...

Every Time I Feel The Spirit

Traditional

2.
I looked around me; it looked so fine;
I asked the Lord if it was mine.
Every time I feel the spirit
Moving in my heart I will pray.
Yes, every time I feel the spirit
Moving in my heart I will pray.

3.
Oh, I have sorrows and I have woe,
And I have heartache here below.
Every time I feel the spirit
Moving in my heart I will pray.
Yes, every time I feel the spirit
Moving in my heart I will pray.

4.
There ain't but one train here on this track.
It runs to heaven, and it don't run back.
Every time I feel the spirit
Moving in my heart I will pray.
Yes, every time I feel the spirit
Moving in my heart I will pray.

5.
But while God leads me I'll never fear,
For I am sheltered by His care.
Every time I feel the spirit
Moving in my heart I will pray.
Yes, every time I feel the spirit
Moving in my heart I will pray.

Gimme That Old Time Religion

Traditional

2.
Gimme that old time religion …
It's good enough for me.
It was good for the Hebrew children,
It was good for the Hebrew children,
It was good for the Hebrew children,
It's good enough for me.

3.
Gimme that old time religion …
It's good enough for me.
It was good for Paul and Silas,
It was good for Paul and Silas,
It was good for Paul and Silas,
It's good enough for me.

4.
Gimme that old time religion …
It's good enough for me.
It was good for our mothers,
It was good for our mothers,
It was good for our mothers,
It's good enough for me.

5.
Gimme that old time religion …
It's good enough for me.
It has saved our fathers,
It has saved our fathers,
It has saved our fathers,
It's good enough for me.

6.
Gimme that old time religion …
It's good enough for me.
It will do when I am dying,
It will do when I am dying,
It will do when I am dying,
It's good enough for me.

7.
Gimme that old time religion …
It's good enough for me.
It will bring you out of bondage,
It will bring you out of bondage,
It will bring you out of bondage,
It's good enough for me.

8.
Gimme that old time religion …
It's good enough for me.
Makes me love everybody,
Makes me love everybody,
Makes me love everybody,
It's good enough for me.

9.
Gimme that old time religion …
It's good enough for me.
It will take us all to heaven,
It will take us all to heaven,
It will take us all to heaven,
It's good enough for me.

Glory, Hallelujah! (John Brown's Body)

Traditional

1. John Brown's — bod - y lies - a - mould - ring in his grave,

John Brown's — bod - y lies a - mould - ring in his grave,

John Brown's — bod - y lies a - mould - ring in his grave, but his

soul goes march - ing on. Glo - ry, glo - ry, hal - le - lu - jah!

Glo - ry, glo - ry, hal - le - lu - jah! Glo - ry, glo - ry, hal - le -

lu - jah! And his soul goes march - ing on.

2.

The stars of heaven are looking kindly down,
The stars of heaven are looking kindly down,
The stars of heaven are looking kindly down
On the grave of old John Brown.
Glory, glory, hallelujah ... on the grave of old John Brown.

3.

He's gone to be a soldier in the army of the Lord,
He's gone to be a soldier in the army of the Lord,
He's gone to be a soldier in the army of the Lord,
And his soul is marching on.
Glory, glory, hallelujah ... and his soul is marching on.

4.

John Brown's knapsack is strapped upon his back,
John Brown's knapsack is strapped upon his back,
John Brown's knapsack is strapped upon his back,
And his soul is marching on.
Glory, glory, hallelujah ... and his soul is marching on.

5.

His pet lambs will meet him on the way,
His pet lambs will meet him on the way,
His pet lambs will meet him on the way,
And they'll go marching on.
Glory, glory, hallelujah ... and they'll go marching on.

6.

They'll hang Jeff Davis to a sour-apple tree,
They'll hang Jeff Davis to a sour-apple tree,
They'll hang Jeff Davis to a sour-apple tree,
And his soul is marching on.
Glory, glory, hallelujah ... and his soul is marching on.

Go Down, Moses

Traditional

1. When Is - rael was in E - gypt - land, —— let my peo - ple go! ——
—— Op - pressed so hard they could not stand, ——
let my peo - ple go! — Go down, —— Mo - ses, ——
way down in E - gypt - land. —————— Tell old ——
Pha - rao —— to let my peo - ple go. ——

2.

Thus spoke the Lord, bold Moses said,
Let my people go!
If not I'll smite your firstborn dead,
Let my people go!
Go down, Moses,
Way down in Egyptland.
Tell old Pharao
To let my people go.

3.

No more shall they in bondage toil,
Let my people go!
Let them come out with Egypt's spoil,
Let my people go!
Go down, Moses,
Way down ...

4.

The Lord told Moses what to do,
Let my people go!
To lead those Hebrew children through,
Let my people go!
Go down, Moses,
Way down ...

5.

Oh, let us all from bondage flee,
Let my people go!
And let us all in Christ be free,
Let my people go!
Go down, Moses,
Way down ...

God Told Hezekiah

Traditional

1. God told He - ze - ki - ah,____ in a mes - sage from on high: "Go set your house in or - der____ for you will sure - ly die."____ He turned to the wall a - weep - ing,____ oh, see the king in tears. He got his bus - i - ness fixed all right,____ God spared him fif - teen years____ Lit - tle black train is a -

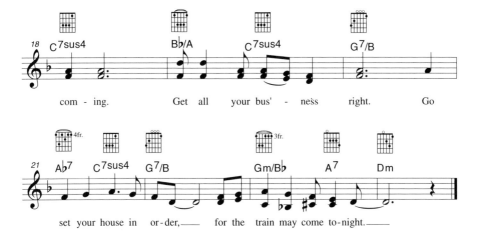

com - ing.   Get all   your bus' - ness   right.   Go

set your house in or - der,___   for the   train may come to-night.___

2.
Go tell that ballroom lady, all filled with wordly pride
That a little black train is coming; get prepared to take a ride.
For the little black train and engine, caboose and baggage car,
And all the folks a-riding got to stop at the jugdement bar.

3.
Did you see that man in darkness, hid from the gospel light?
Did you hear him scream for mercy when the train came moving in sight?
The devil had him in shackles, wrapped around his soul so tight,
No time to fix his business when the train rolled in that night.

Good News! The Chariot's Comin'

Traditional

2.
There's a pair of wings in the heaven, I know.
There's a pair of wings in the heaven, I know.
There's a pair of wings in the heaven, I know,
And I don't want it to leave me behind.

3.
There's a pair of shoes in the heaven, I know.
There's a pair of shoes in the heaven, I know.
There's a pair of shoes in the heaven, I know,
And I don't want it to leave me behind.

4.
There's a starry crown in the heaven, I know.
There's a starry crown in the heaven, I know.
There's a starry crown in the heaven, I know,
And I don't want it to leave me behind.

5.
There's a golden harp in the heaven, I know.
There's a golden harp in the heaven, I know.
There's a golden harp in the heaven, I know,
And I don't want it to leave me behind.

Hallelu', Hallelu'

Traditional

Hal - le - lu', hal - le - lu', hal - le - lu', hal - le - lu - jah, praise ye the Lord! Hal - le - Lord 1. Praise ye the Lord, hal - le - lu - jah, praise ye the Lord, hal - le - lu - jah, praise ye the Lord, hal - le - lu - jah, praise ye the Lord!

2.	3.	4.
Preiset den Herrn, hallelujah,	Gloire au Seigneur, hallelujah,	Doxa theou, hallelujah,
Preiset den Herrn, hallelujah,	Gloire au Seigneur, hallelujah,	Doxa theou, hallelujah,
Preiset den Herrn, hallelujah,	Gloire au Seigneur, hallelujah,	Doxa theou, hallelujah,
Preiset den Herrn!	Gloire au Seigneur!	Doxa theou!
(German/allemand/deutsch)	(French/français/französisch)	(Greek/grec/griechisch)

Have You Got Good Religion

Traditional

Have you got good re-li-gion?____

Cer-tain-ly, Lord!____ Have you got good re-li-gion?____

Cer-tain-ly, Lord!____ Have you got good re-li - gion?

Cer-tain-ly, Lord!_____ Cer-tain-ly, cer-tain-ly,

1., 2.

cer-tain-ly, Lord!____

3.

Cer-tain-ly Lord!_____

2.
Have you been baptized? Certainly...

3.
Did you go to the valley? ...

4.
Did you get on your knees? ...

5.
Did your soul get ease? ...

Heaven

Traditional

I got shoes,— you got shoes,— all God's chil-dren got shoes, my Lord.— When I get to heav-en, gon-na put on them shoes, - I'm gon-na walk, yeah,— walk, yeah,— I'm gon-na walk— all o-ver God's heav-en, yeah,— Lord, heav-en, yeah,— Lord, heav-en, Lord!— Ev'-ry-bo-dy's talk-in' of but

no one's ev - er go - in' to heav - en, yeah,_____ Lord,

heav - en, Lord!_____ I'm gon - na walk all o - ver God's

heav - en, oh, yeah!_____

2. I got a robe, you got a robe,
All God's children got robes, my Lord.
When I get to heaven gonna wear that robe,
I'm gonna shout, yeah, shout, yeah,
I'm gonna shout all over God's heaven, yeah, Lord,
heaven, yeah, Lord, heaven, Lord!
Ev'rybody's talkin' of but no one's ever goin' to heaven,
yeah, Lord, heaven, Lord!
I'm gonna shout all over God's heaven, oh, yeah!

3. I got wings, you got wings,
All God's children got wings, my Lord.
When I get to heaven gonna use them wings,
I'm gonna fly, yeah, fly, yeah,
I'm gonna fly all over God's heaven, yeah, Lord,
heaven, yeah, Lord, heaven, Lord!
Ev'rybody's talkin' of but no one's ever goin' to heaven,
yeah, Lord, heaven, Lord!
I'm gonna fly all over God's heaven, oh, yeah!

Heaven Is So High

Traditional

Heav-en is so high you can't get o-ver it, so low you can't get un-der it, so wide you can't get a-round it; you must come in at the door. 1. You might as well just make up your mind. You must come in at the door. Broth-er soon-er or la-ter you're bound to find, you must come in at the door.

Fine

D.C. al Fine

2.
There's only one path that takes you there,
It leads right up to the door.
It's narrow and straight but it's free from care,
You must come in at the door.

Heaven is so high ...

3.
If you get there before I do,
You must come in at the door.
Don't worry, don't wait, I'm coming, too,
You must come in at the door.

Heaven is so high ...

4.
You'll find it's always open wide,
You must come in at the door.
So, brother, don't stop till you're inside,
You must come in at the door.

Heaven is so high ...

He's Got The Whole World In His Hands

Traditional

2.
He's got the tiny little baby in his hands,
…
He's got the whole world in his hands.

3.
He's got you and me, brother, in his hands,
…
He's got the whole world in his hands.

4.
He's got the son and his father in his hands,
…
He's got the whole world in his hands.

5.
He's got the mother and her daughter in his hands,
…
He's got the whole world in his hands.

6.
He's got everybody here in his hands,
…
He's got the whole world in his hands.

7.
He's got the sun and the moon in his hands,
…
He's got the whole world in his hands.

8.
He's got the whole world in his hands,
…
He's got the whole world in his hands.

I Am Weak, But Thou Are Strong

(Just A Closer Walk With Thee)

Traditional

I'll Fly Away

Traditional

Some bright morn-ing when this life is o-ver, I'll fly a-way. To a home on God's ce-les-tial lad-der, I'll fly a-way. I'll fly a-way, oh glo-ry, I'll fly a-way in the morn-ing. When I die, hal-le-lu-jah, by and by. I'll fly a-way.

If I Could I Surely Would
(Oh Mary, Don't You Weep)

Traditional

1. If I could ___ I sure - ly would ___ stand on the rock where Mo - ses stood. ___ Pha - raoh's ar - my got drown - ded, oh Ma - ry, don't you weep. Oh Ma - ry, don't you weep, don't you mourn, oh Ma - ry, don't you weep, don't you mourn. Pha - raoh's ar - my got drown - ded, oh Ma - ry, don't you weep.

2.
Moses stood on the Red Sea shore,
Smotin' the water with a two-by-four.
Pharao's army ...

3.
The Lord told Moses what to do
To lead those Hebrew children through.
Pharao's army ...

If You Want Joy

Traditional

If you want joy, re-al joy, won-der-ful joy, let Je-sus come in-to your heart! If you want heart! Your sins He'll take a-way, your night He'll turn to day, your life He'll make o-ver a-new and then come in to stay: If you want joy, re-al joy, won-der-ful joy, let Je-sus come in-to your heart!

I'm Gonna Sing

Traditional

1. I'm gon - na sing when the spir - it says   sing.   I'm gon - na

sing when the spir - it says   sing.—   I'm gon - na sing when the spir - it says

sing,   and o - bey   the spir - it of the   Lord!

2. I'm gonna shout when the spirit says shout …
… And obey the spirit of the Lord.

3. I'm gonna preach when the spirit says preach …
… And obey the spirit of the Lord.

4. I'm gonna pray when the spirit says pray …
… And obey the spirit of the Lord.

5. I'm gonna sing when the spirit says sing …
… And obey the spirit of the Lord.

Joshua Fit The Battle Of Jericho

Traditional

2.
Joshua fit ...
Up to the walls of Jericho,
He marches with spear in hand;
Go, blow that ram horns, Joshua cried,
Cause the battle is in my hand.

3.
Joshua fit ...Then the lamb ram sheep horns
begin to blow,
Trumpets begin to sound,
Joshua commanded the children to shout,
And the walls come tumbling down.

© 2003 Schott Musik International, Mainz

49

It Is Me
(Standin' In The Need For Prayer)

Traditional

It is me, it is me, it is me, oh Lord, stand-in' in the need of prayer. It is me, it is me, it is me, oh Lord, stand-in' in the need of prayer. *Fine* 1. Not my moth-er, not my fa-ther, it is me, oh Lord, stand-in' in the need of

prayer,   not my   moth-er, not my   fa-ther, it   is   me,   oh

Lord,   stand-in' in the   need   of   prayer.

D.C. al Fine

2.

Not my brother, not my sister, it is me, oh Lord,
Standin' in the need for prayer.

3.

Not my teacher, not my preacher, it is me, oh Lord,
Standin' in the need for prayer.

Kum ba yah

Traditional

Kum ba yah, my Lord, kum ba yah. Kum ba
yah, my Lord, kum ba yah. Kum ba yah, my Lord, kum ba
yah. Oh Lord, ———— kum ba yah.

2.

Someone's singing, Lord, kum ba yah …

3.

Someone's shouting, Lord, kum ba yah …

4.

Someone's praying, Lord, kum ba yah …

5.

Someone's weeping, Lord, kum ba yah …

Lord, I Want To Be A Christian

Traditional

2.
Lord, I want to be more loving in-a my heart,
In-a my heart,
Lord, I want to be more loving in-a my heart.
In-a my heart, in-a my heart …

3.
Lord, I want to be more holy in-a my heart,
In-a my heart,
Lord, I want to be more holy in-a my heart.
In-a my heart, in-a my heart …

54

Let Me Fly

Traditional

2.

I got a mother in the promised land,
Ain't gonna stop until I shake her hand.
Not so particular 'bout shakin' her hand,
But I just wanna go up in the promised land.
Now let me fly …

3.

Meet that hypocrite on the street,
First thing he'll do is to show his teeth.
Next thing he'll do is to tell a lie,
And the best thing to do is to pass him by.
Now let me fly …

4.

The sun that bids us rest is waking our
Brethren 'neath the western sky; and hour
By hour fresh lips are making Thy
Wondrous doings heard on high.
Now let me fly …

5.

So be it, Lord, Thy throne shall never,
Like earth's proud empires, pass away;
Thy kingdom stands and grows for ever,
Till all Thy creatures own Thy sway.
Now let me fly …

Listen To The Lambs

Traditional

give you a crown,—— want to go to heav-en when I die. O,

2.
Mind out brother how you walk the course,
Want to go to heaven when I die.
Your foot might slip and your soul get lost,
Want to go to heaven when I die.

Listen to the lambs ...

3.
Come on, mourner, and don't be ,shamed,
Want to go to heaven when I die.
The angel's waitin' for to write out your name,
Want to go to heaven when I die.

Listen to the lambs ...

Mary And Martha

Traditional

1. Ma - ry and Mar - tha just gone 'long, Ma - ry and Mar - tha just gone 'long, Ma - ry and Mar - tha just gone 'long to ring them charm - ing bells. Cry - in': "Free grace and un - dy - in' love,

free grace and un - dy - in' love, free grace and un -

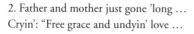

dy - in' love", to ring them charm - ing bells.

2. Father and mother just gone 'long …
Cryin': "Free grace and undyin' love …

3. Brother and sister just gone 'long …
Cryin': "Free grace and undyin' love …

4. Preacher and elder just gone 'long …
Cryin': "Free grace and undyin' love …

5. Everybody just gone 'long …
Cryin': "Free grace and undyin' love …

Michael, Row The Boat Ashore

Traditional

2. Michael, boat a gospel boat, hallelujah …

3. Brother, lend a helping hand, hallelujah …

4. Sister, help to trim the sail, hallelujah …

5. Sinner, row to save your soul, hallelujah …

6. Boastful talk will sink your soul, hallelujah …

7. Gabriel, blow the trumpet horn, hallelujah …

8. Jordan stream is deep and wide, hallelujah …

9. Jesus stand on the other side, hallelujah …

More And More

Traditional

Oh Freedom

Traditional

2.
No more moaning, no more moaning,
No more moaning over me, over me.
And before I'll be a slave …

3.
No more crying, no more crying,
No more crying over me, over me.
And before I'll be a slave …

4.
There'll be singing, there'll be singing,
There'll be singing over me, over me.
And before I'll be a slave …

My Lord, What A Morning

Traditional

2. You'll hear the sinner mourn,
To wake the nations underground,
Looking to my God's right hand,
When the stars begin to fall.

3. You'll hear the Christian shout,
To wake the nations underground,
Looking to my God's right hand,
When the stars begin to fall.

4. Oh, father, what will you do,
To wake the nations underground,
Looking to my God's right hand,
When the stars begin to fall.

5. Oh, mother, what will you do,
To wake the nations underground,
Looking to my God's right hand,
When the stars begin to fall.

6. Oh, brother, what will you do,
To wake the nations underground,
Looking to my God's right hand,
When the stars begin to fall.

7. Oh, sister, what will you do,
To wake the nations underground,
Looking to my God's right hand,
When the stars begin to fall.

8. I'll bid farewell to this old world,
To wake the nations underground,
Looking to my God's right hand,
When the stars begin to fall.

9. I'll go home to the gloryland,
To wake the nations underground,
Looking to my God's right hand,
When the stars begin to fall.

Easy Version

Traditional

Nobody Knows The Trouble I've Seen

2.
Although you see me going 'long so. Oh, yes Lord.
I have my trials here below. Oh, yes Lord.

3.
One day when I was walking 'long. Oh, yes Lord.
The elements opened and His love came down. Oh,
yes Lord.

4.
I never shall forget that day. Oh yes, Lord.
When Jesus washed my sins away. Oh yes, Lord.

5.
What makes old Satan hate me so? Oh yes, Lord.
'Cause he got me once and let me go. Oh yes, Lord.

6.
Oh, every day to You I pray. Oh yes, Lord.
For you to drive my sins away. Oh yes, Lord.

Nobody Knows The Trouble I've Seen

Traditional

1. No - bod - y knows the trou - ble I've seen,

no - bod - y knows but Je - sus. No - bod - y knows the

trou - ble I've seen, glo - ry hal - le - lu - jah. Some -

times I'm up, some - times I'm down. Oh, yes Lord. Some -

times I'm al - most to the ground. Oh, yes Lord.

For additional lyrics see page 65.

Oh, Father Abraham

Traditional

Oh Happy Day

Traditional

Oh hap-py day, oh hap-py day

when Je-sus washed, oh when he washed,

when Je-sus washed, he washed my

sin a-way. Oh hap-py day, oh hap-py

day. 1. He taught me how to
and live en - joy - ing ev'ry-

Oh, My Soul, My Soul
(Angel Gabriel)

Traditional

1. Oh, my soul, my soul is a - going for to rest in the

arms of the an - gel Ga - bri - el, and I climb on a hill and I

look to the west, and I cross o - ver Jor - dan to the lamb; and I'll

sit me down in the old arm - chair; oh,___ broth - ers, I will nev - er

tire, and old Sa - tan may sneeze, but I will take my ease, and I'll

2. Oh, my soul, my soul is a-going for to rest
Going to rest just as sure as I am born,
And I'll look like a blackbird a-sitting on a nest
When old Gabriel is blowing on the horn;
And I'll leave my clothes safe upon the shore,
For I'll have new garments for to wear;
And I'll have brand-new shoes and never get the blues,
and the angels they will come and curl my hair.

I will shout …

Oh, Sinner Man

Traditional

1. Oh, sin - ner man where you gon - na run to?
2. Run to the rock, the rock, it was melt - ing.

Oh, sin - ner man, where you gon - na run to? Oh, sin - ner man,
Run to the rock, the rock, it was melt - ing. Run to the rock,

where you gon - na run to all on that day?
the rock, it was melt - ing all on that day.

3. Run to the sea, the sea, it was boiling ...
All on that day.

4. Run to the moon, the moon, it was bleeding ...
All on that day.

5. Run to the Lord. "Lord, won't you hide me?" ...
All on that day.

6. Run to the devil, the devil was waiting ...
All on that day.

7. Oh, sinner man, you ought to have been praying ...
All on that day.

Oh, When The Saints

Traditional

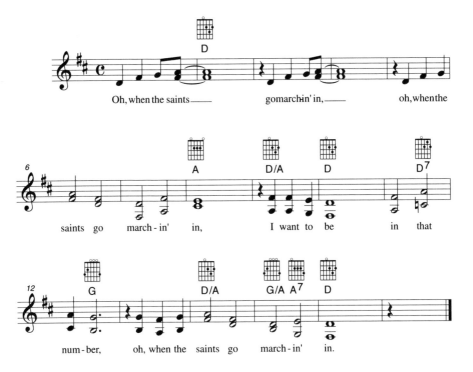

Oh, when the saints___ go marchin' in,___ oh, when the
saints go march-in' in, I want to be in that
num-ber, oh, when the saints go march-in' in.

2.
And when the stars begin to shine,
And when the stars begin to shine,
I want to be in that number,
Oh, when the stars begin to shine.

3.
When Gabriel blows in his horn, ...

4.
And when the band begins to play, ...

5.
And when the sun refuse to shine, ...

6.
And when they gather round the throne, ...

7.
And when they crown him King of Kings,
...

8.
And on that hallelujah-day, ...

⁷⁴ Oh, The Foxes Have Holes In The Ground
(Hard Trials)

Traditional

Oh, the fox - es have holes in the ground, and the birds have their nests in the air, and ev' - ry - thing has a hid - den place but us poor sin - ners ain't got no - where. Now aint't them hard tri - als, great trib - u - la - tions,___ hard tri - als, hard tri - als I am bound to leave___ this land.___ You may go this way,___ you may

Oh, Won't You Sit Down

Traditional

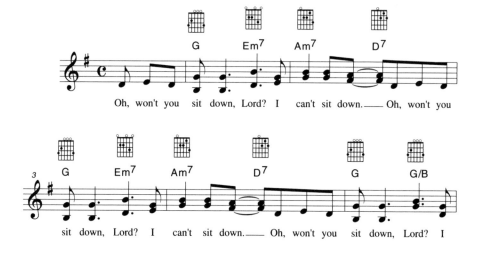

Oh, won't you sit down, Lord? I can't sit down.— Oh, won't you

sit down, Lord? I can't sit down.— Oh, won't you sit down, Lord? I

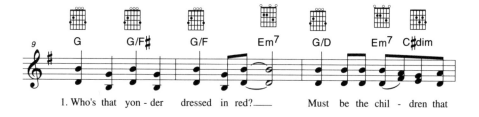

can't sit down,— 'cause I just got to heav-en, got to look a-round.—

1. Who's that yon-der dressed in red?— Must be the chil-dren that

2.
Who's that yonder dressed in blue?
Must be the children that are comin' through.
Who's that yonder dressed in black?
Must be the hypocrites a-turnin' back.

Oh, won't you sit down, Lord? I can't sit down ...

Oh, You Got Jesus
(One More River To Cross)

Traditional

1. Oh, you got Je - sus, hold him fast, — one more riv - er to
good old cha - riot pass - ing by, — one more ri - ver to

cross. Oh, bet - ter love was nev - er told, — one more riv-er to
cross. She jarred the earth and shook the sky, — one more ri - ver to—

cross. Oh, cross. Oh, was-n't that a wide riv - er,
— 2. The cross.

riv - er of Jor - dan, Lord, wide——— riv - er, there's

one more riv - er to cross. Oh, was - n't that a cross.

Rise And Shine

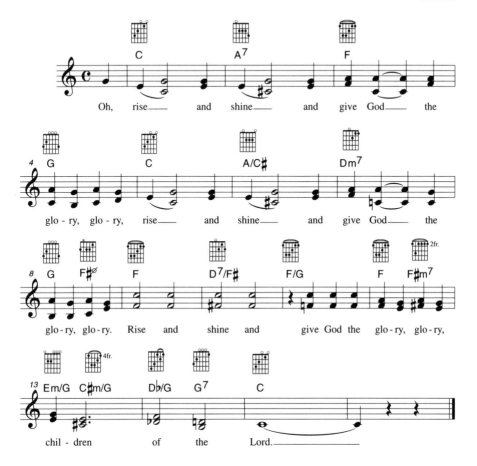

Traditional

Oh, rise—— and shine—— and give God—— the
glo-ry, glo-ry, rise—— and shine—— and give God—— the
glo-ry, glo-ry. Rise and shine and give God the glo-ry, glo-ry,
chil-dren of the Lord.——

2. The Lord said: "Noah, there's gonna be a floody, floody."
Lord said: "Noah, there's gonna be a floody, floody.
Get your children out of the muddy, muddy,
Children of the Lord."

3. So Noah, he went out and he built an arky, arky,
Noah, he went out and he built an arky, arky.
Made it out of hickory barky, barky,
Children of the Lord.

4. The animals, they came and went in by twosy, twosy,
Animals, they came and went in by twosy, twosy.
Elephants and kangoroosy, roosy,
Children of the Lord.

5. It rained and rained for forty daysy, daysy,
Rained and rained for forty daysy, daysy.
Drove those animals nearly crazy, crazy,
Children of the Lord.

Over In The Gloryland

Traditional

Way o - ver in the glo - ry - land,

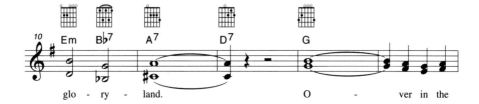

see that hap-py an - gel - band, o - ver in the

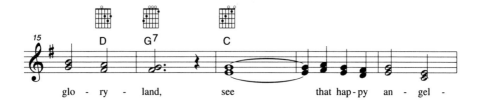

glo - ry - land. O - ver in the

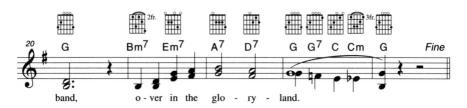

glo - ry - land, see that hap-py an - gel -

band, o - ver in the glo - ry - land.

Fine

1. Sin-ners, there are rocks a-head, don't for-get what Je-sus said, o-ver in the glo-ry - land. Wan-na walk through heav-en's door, bow your head and sin no more, o - ver in the glo - ry - land.

2.
Sometimes when I'm all alone,
Dream of my eternal home,
Over in the gloryland.
Can't be long now till I'm there,
Peace and mercy everywhere,
Over in the gloryland.

Way over in the gloryland …

3.
Sinner, don't you hide your face,
If you wanna see that place,
Over in the gloryland.
Sure ain't got no time to lose,
If it's goin' that you choose,
Over in the gloryland.

Way over in the gloryland …

Rock My Soul

Traditional

Rock my soul in the bos - om of A - bra - ham,

rock my soul in the bos - om of A - bra - ham, rock my soul in the

bos - om of A - bra - ham, oh, rock - a my soul.

So high I can't get o - ver it, so low I

can't get un - der it, so wide I can't get 'round____ of it,

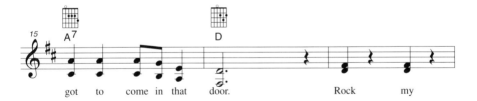

got   to   come   in   that   door.   Rock   my

soul,   rock   my   soul,   rock   my

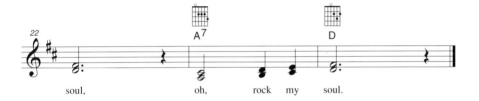

soul,   oh,   rock   my   soul.

Roll, Jordan, Roll

Traditional

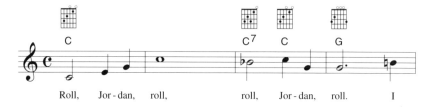

Roll, Jor - dan, roll, roll, Jor - dan, roll. I

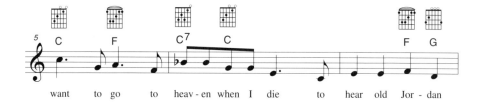

want to go to heav - en when I die to hear old Jor - dan

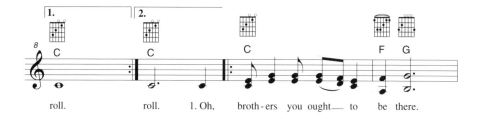

roll. roll. 1. Oh, broth - ers you ought — to be there.

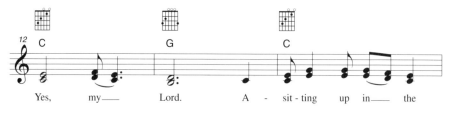

Yes, my — Lord. A - sit - ting up in — the

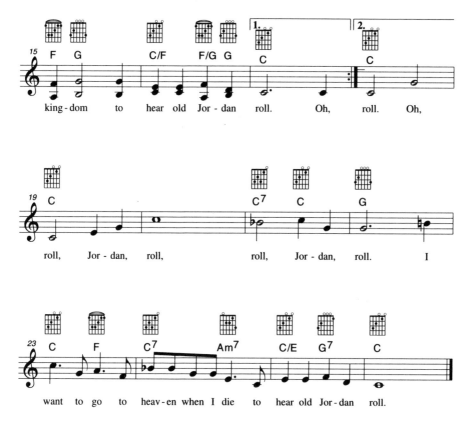

2.
Oh, sisters, you ought to be there.
Yes, my Lord.
A-sitting up in the kingdom
To hear old Jordan roll.
Oh, sisters, you ought to be there.
Yes, my Lord.
A-sitting up in the kingdom
To hear old Jordan roll.

Oh, roll, Jordan, roll …

3.
Oh, sinner, you ought to be there.
Yes, my Lord.
A-sitting up in the kingdom
To hear old Jordan roll.
Oh, sinner, you ought to be there.
Yes, my Lord.
A-sitting up in the kingdom
To hear old Jordan roll.

Oh, roll, Jordan, roll …

Singin' With A Sword In My Hand

Traditional

87

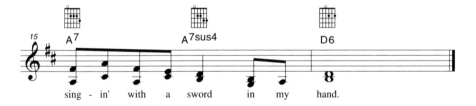

sing - in' with a sword in my hand.

2.
Shoutin' with a sword in my hand, Lord,
Shoutin' with a sword in my hand.
Purtiest shoutin' ever I heard way over on
the hill.
The angels shout and I shout, too.
Shoutin' with a sword in my hand, Lord,
Shoutin' with a sword in my hand,
In my hand, Lord, shoutin' with a sword in
my hand.

4.
Prayin' with a sword in my hand, Lord,
Prayin' with a sword in my hand.
Purtiest prayin' ever I heard way over on the
hill.
The angels pray and I pray, too.
Prayin' with a sword in my hand, Lord,
Prayin' with a sword in my hand,
In my hand, Lord, prayin' with a sword in
my hand.

3.
Preachin' with a sword in my hand, Lord,
Preachin' with a sword in my hand.
Purtiest preachin' ever I heard way over on
the hill.
The angels preach and I preach, too.
Preachin' with a sword in my hand, Lord,
Preachin' with a sword in my hand,
In my hand, Lord, preachin' with a sword in
my hand.

5.
Mournin' with a sword in my hand, Lord,
Mournin' with a sword in my hand.
Purtiest mournin' ever I heard way over on
the hill.
The angels mourn and I mourn, too.
Mournin' with a sword in my hand, Lord,
Mournin' with a sword in my hand,
In my hand, Lord, mournin' with a sword in
my hand.

Somebody's Knockin' At Your Door

Traditional

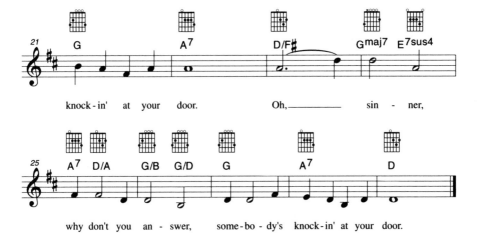

knock - in' at your door.   Oh,_____ sin - ner,

why don't you an - swer,   some - bo - dy's knock - in' at your door.

2.
Answer Jesus!
Somebody's knockin' at your door.
Answer Jesus!
Somebody's knockin' at your door.
Oh, sinner, why don't you answer?
Somebody's knockin' at your door.

Sometimes I Feel Like A Motherless Child

Traditional

2.
Sometimes I feel like I'm almost gone,
Sometimes I feel like I'm almost gone,
Sometimes I feel like I'm almost gone,
Way up in the heavenly land,
Way up in the heavenly land.
True believer!
Way up in the heavenly land,
Way up in the heavenly land.

3.
Sometimes I feel like a feather in the air,
Sometimes I feel like a feather in the air,
Sometimes I feel like a feather in the air,
And I spread my wings and I fly,
I spread my wings and I fly.
True believer!
And I spread my wings and I fly,
I spread my wings and I fly.

Steal Away

Traditional

1. Steal a - way, steal a - way, steal a - way to Je - sus.
Steal a - way, steal a - way home. I ain't got long to stay here.
My Lord___ calls me, He calls me by the thun - der; the
trum-pet___ sounds with - in___ my soul! I ain't got long to stay here.

2.
Steal away, steal away,
steal away to Jesus.
Steal away, steal away home.
I ain't got long to stay here.

Green trees a-bending,
Poor sinner stands a-trembling;
The trumpet sounds within my soul!
I ain't got long to stay here.

This Train Is Bound For Glory

Traditional

1. This train is bound for glo-ry, this train. ____

This train is bound for glo-ry, this train. ____

This train is bound for glo-ry, don't ride noth-in' but the

right-eous and the ho-ly. This train is bound for glo-ry, this train. ____

2.
This train don't pull no gamblers, this train ...
No hypocrites and no midnight ramblers,
This train is bound for glory, this train.

3.
This train don't pull no jokers, this train ...
No cigarette puffers and no cigar smokers ...

4.
This train don't pull no dancers, this train ...
No hootchie-cootch shakers and no charleston prancers ...

5.
This train don't pull no rustlers, this train ...
No sidestreet walkers and no two-bit hustlers ...

6.
This train don't pull no liars, this train ...
No hypocrites and no high flyers ...

7.
This train don't pull no extras, this train ...
Don't pull nothing but the heavenly special...

8.
This train is built for speed now, this train ...
Fastest train that you ever did see, ...

Swing Low, Sweet Chariot

Traditional

com - in' for to car - ry me home.

2.
If you get there before I do,
Comin' for to carry me home,
Tell all my friends I'm comin', too,
Comin' for to carry me home.

Swing low, sweet chariot,
Comin' for to carry me home.
Swing low, sweet chariot,
comin' for to carry me home.

3.
The brightest day that ever I saw,
Comin' for to carry me home,
When Jesus washed my sins away,
Comin' for to carry me home.

Swing low, sweet chariot,
Comin' for to carry me home.
Swing low, sweet chariot,
comin' for to carry me home.

4.
I ain't never been to heaven but I been told,
Comin' for to carry me home,
That the streets in heaven are paved with gold,
Comin' for to carry me home.

Swing low, sweet chariot,
Comin' for to carry me home.
Swing low, sweet chariot,
comin' for to carry me home.

5.
I'm sometimes up and sometimes down,
Comin' for to carry me home,
But still my soul feels heavenly bound,
Comin' for to carry me home.

Swing low, sweet chariot,
Comin' for to carry me home.
Swing low, sweet chariot,
comin' for to carry me home.

The Angel Rolled The Stone Away

Traditional

The an - gel rolled the stone a - way;

the an - gel rolled the stone a - way,

'twas on a bright and shin - y morn when the

trum - pet be - gan to sound. The an - gel rolled the

stone a - way. 1. Sis - ter Ma - ry came a -

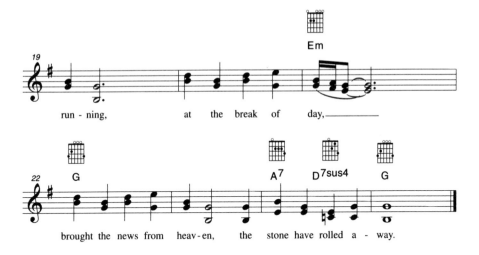

run - ning,   at   the   break   of   day,———

brought the news from   heav-en,   the   stone have rolled a - way.

2.
I'm a-looking for my Savior,
Tell me where He lay
High upon the mountain,
The stone have rolled away.

3.
The soldiers there a-plenty,
Standing by the door,
But they could not hinder
The stone have rolled away.

4.
Old Pilate and his wise men
Didn't know what to say,
The miracle was on them,
The stone have rolled away.

Wade In The Water

Traditional

Wade in the wa - ter.— Wade in the wa-ter, chil - dren.
Wade in the wa - ter.— God's to trou - ble the
wa - ter.— 1. See that band all dressed in— white.—
God's goin' to trou-ble the wa - ter.— The lead - er looks like the
Is - rael-ite.— God's goin' to trou-ble the wa - ter.—

2.
See that band all dressed in red.
God's goin' to trouble the water.
Looks like the band that Moses lead.
God's goin' to trouble the water.

3.
Remember one thing that's certainly sure.
God's goin' to trouble the water.
Judgement's comin' and I don't know.
God's goin' to trouble the water.

4.
Upon the mountain Jehova spoke.
God's goin' to trouble the water.
Out of His mouth came fire and smoke.
God's goin' to trouble the water.

5.
I heard a rumblin' up in the sky.
God's goin' to trouble the water.
Must have been Jesus passin' by.
God's goin' to trouble the water.

6.
Down in the valley, down on my knees.
God's goin' to trouble the water.
Askin' my Lord in heaven will hear my prayer.
God's goin' to trouble the water.

7.
You can hinder me here,
You can hinder me there.
God's goin' to trouble the water.
But the Lord in heaven will hear my prayer.
God's goin' to trouble the water.

8.
The enemy's great, but my Captain's strong.
God's goin' to trouble the water.
I'm marchin' to the city and the road ain't long.
God's goin' to trouble the water.

Oh, By And By

Traditional

1. Oh, by and by,_____ by and by,_____ I'm goin' to lay down my heav-y load._____ I know my robe's goin' to fit me well,_____ I'm goin' to lay down my heav-y load._____ I tried it on at the gates of hell,_____ I'm goin' to lay down my heav-y load._____

2. Oh, by and by, by and by,
I'm goin' to lay down my heavy load.
Oh, hell is deep and dark's despair,
I'm goin' to lay down my heavy load,
Oh, stop poor sinner and don't go there.
I'm goin' to lay down my heavy load.